Berli
A Bottle F

Christopher Sanderson
A Coastmoor Publication

A Ten Or Twenty Pence Poems Imprint

ISBN: 9798685833464

To John & Sheri

CHRISTMAS 2020

Be a visionary.

These are poems written with a Lamy fountain pen
using the very same

Unique fountain pen ink composition by the contemporary painter Viktor Walter.

*This fountain pen ink was developed to work best with the recycled paper used
in the original Berlin Notebook. However, it looks good on a regular copy paper
too.*

These are poems written on the very same recycled
paper now to be found in Berlin Notebook *Nummer
Eins*

Would the blue be any bluer
With the use of Berlin Blue ink
Would the melancholy be any deeper
With the sense to stop and think

Would we all still be fighting
To pay the outstanding credit card bill
Would the charges be in keeping
With the thoughts which we all instil

Now that I write in blue
Will I, necessarily
Move closer to you
With my ink from Berlin
And my pen from France
Will we each see within
To decide upon our next dance

Will the new notebook
Limit our outpouring
Should we see a deeper look
As our certainties are soaring
Shall the fourteen lines
Become the favoured form
To once more settle your designs

The Blue Pen is our symbol
It is our object
For it writes of our love
If not quite so uneasily
As it writes of our loss

It holds this presence
On the cusp
Straddling the happiness
And the unhappiness
With the same sorrows and joys

The Blue Pen is our reflection
Of raspberries, blueberries
Days in meadows, or
Days walking on the moor
Cooling our feet in the stream

I love the blue
But also
The strawberry yoghurt
Yes, the ink filled fountain pen
But equally
The 16 billion live cultures

I love for the record
And
The Soul of Carmen Miranda
I love the playlist songs
Along with
Their exposures of the spirit

I love the chair in which I sit
As
I drink my pot of tea
I love how my mind wanders
When
I imagine how the verse rises and falls

I follow a love
Which, for the sake of truth
Cannot be defeated

I follow a love
Which, for the sake of beauty
Cannot be impeded

How so wildly irresistible
The love of truth
How undeniably irresistible
The love of beauty

I cannot be defeated
If I follow a love
For the sake of truth

I cannot be impeded
If I follow a love
For the sake of beauty

Sunlight
On stone flags
Truth, beauty, and love
The whole damned thing
In that one sunlit instant

Moonlight
On rippled sands
Hopes, expectations, and desires
The whole gambit
In that one moonlit moment

Spotlight
On the poet's face
Implants, extractions, and retouches
The whole portfolio
In that one spotlit consultation

I court the evening primrose once more
When days are good
I firm my back against my bench
I say not to rhyme, but maybe I should

Every day there is a birthday
Today it is Grandson Benjamin's day
Every day there is the sunshine
From the smile as he turns to play

I court the lunchtime perfume
In search of love of grace
I bend my back in my armchair
I may not rhyme, but maybe will give chase

Where are the ones we love
In our mind, and in our heart
In our body, in our soul
Where are the ones worthy to chart

I see the still water
I need only to write the poem
I see the calm surface
I need only to write for you

For you
To see the still water
For you
To see the calm surface

I am in the mid-afternoon
Still water on through dusk
I am in the month of the summer
Calm surface on into the night

For you
To see on through dusk
For you
To see on into the night

The blue nib
Reels out the rhythms
The blue pen
Takes them as they come

There on the shadow
The penetration
Or the layer
Takes on a new meaning

Then, a few overs later
The fifth wicket falls
So, now the danger
Of a result exists

With a shared love of the game
The commentators
Are coupled together
With their appreciative listeners

I write for my own song
As I listen to another's song
I write to catch hold of my own morning
After reading the poetry of a master

I write in blue
For the love of Berlin
Yet, having not ever been there
I write in shadows

Although I do know of the Buddhist Monastery
Also of the Chamäleon Theatre
And the bars
Where unique whiskies are served

And I know of imagined love
Of kisses, on the bridge
Across the river
On the way back to our hotel rooms

My knee bounces
After two or three notes
My foot taps
On an imaginary dance floor

I am listening
To *Chinese Envoy* by John Cage
All of the metaphors are used
To make the sound resonate

I love the song
I love the joy
Which my heart, and my knee
And my feet, all feel for this music

After bouncing
I turn to melancholy
After love
I turn to life

My Berlin Blue ink
Released onto the page by
My Lamy clear-barrelled pen

Its nib to scratch
On my notebook's
Recycled paper

The world is
Multi-national
As I write this

I think of the poem
About a *red wheelbarrow*
By someone I don't remember

He, or she
Made their name
With I know not

What kind of ink
Or if a fountain pen even, no
Perhaps they would have used a pencil

This pen, with Berlin Blue ink
Allows the essence of my life
To pour out from my soul
Or my spirit as some might name it

The nib and the cartridge
The barrel and the cap
They all come together
To unlock the flow of today's waves

Sunlight through the crystals
Trees, blown by a vigorous breeze
Even a wind you could say
On this otherwise quiet Sunday morning

Before the cricket begins
Before stumps and bails
Are set up to be bowled at
Life, to be knocked over

Only to be rebuilt again
Once the scorecard is completed

Peter Green's Fleetwood Mac
Took me to the blues back in 1967
Rest in peace Peter

Berlin ink and my Lamy pen
Take me to the blues in 2020
Rest in peace the years in between

Fifty-three years of a life
With sexual gratification at its core
If you don't mind me saying so

I have to leave, you should know why
Shall I tell you about my life
It will keep you amused I'm sure

Would you like single beds
Or would a double be ok
I don't mind, you choose

From the beginning, and then to about mid-way
Now we just repeat the words
So that the pen may write

It is my responsibility
Not a word I use easily
Or often

But with things being
As they were
I had to stand up for myself

Not that I know with any certainty
What the action will be
Which follows my decision

The breeze has died down
The trees still wave about
If now ever so slightly

Similarly the mind
After a small nap following Beethoven
Is somewhat settled

The memory
Is of the stream on the moor
Sat on the grass, apart from the world

So the question is
How to repeat the process
Which so so surely takes one to freedom

Heartbeat in blue
One name not given
One name not shown
Heartbeat sown in blue

The crystal disseminates
Sunlight to all corners
With its circular globe

The wind blows willingly
To the furthest reaches
Of the gardens trees

Heartbeat in blue
One place not owned
One place not returned
Heartbeat, earnest in blue

I am with you
As if I am with myself
I write in Berlin Blue
From the cupboard with the shelf

I try to remain true
Through my fading wealth
I scope the ways in blue
For my mind's unknown inner health

I take what I think is due
I do it though lacking stealth
Skipping along the lines of winding blue
I am in search of a surer self

I weave about the all day through
On the road, from here onto oneself
A carrier for the ink of blue
Before I return you, truly, to my other self

Was it not blue
Which brought love
From Prussia
To Yves Klein
With the now famous turquoise

Or was it a darker blue
A blacker blue
Which led me on
Which set my mind thinking
Thoughts what it ought not to think

Such that now
This blue of the moment
Cannot express
Those deeper convictions
Which the eyes once fell upon

Forever summer
Chopin and Chardin
And my long lasting
Love of blue
My love
Trimmed round by you

Forever Autumn
Oslo and Vienna
And my deep casting
Love of blue
My love
Skimmed through by you

Forever winter
Dark and light
And my never fasting
Love of blue
My love
Brimmed over by you

That day
Which I don't, in its entirety
Regret
May well have signalled
The beginning, in all likelihood
Of the blue

That I don't
Have a clear reflection, or retention
Is unfortunate
But don't let's pretend
That they were not good times
From that day forwards

The blue was among us
Not being disrespectful
Yet neither celebrating
Not in the way
That on that particular day
We might, rightfully, have expected

In anticipation of your next question
As I move from blue to blue
With the sense of resurrection
Or our belief in, yes, me too

Each and every day
The tree wavers and wobbles
As the ever so slight breeze works
Its way through the many thousand leaves

How then to reconcile the thoughts
Which got me this far, or which
Asked that I rise from my book
To find a new place for the writing

And if there is to be no reconciliation
From the one thought to the next
How might yesterday fare
On the scale of worthwhile memories

Would things be more impressive
With a good measure of solitude
Might that then be the answer, on which
You would care for me to contemplate

Why not go on retreat
To Gladstone's library
Or another quiet place
For literary inspiration

Simply choose a place
With access
To a load of books
Of your kind of choosing

Find a bed, and a room
With comfort
Its leading priority
Also, a place close by to write

Why not go on retreat
To your home
Make it that other place
For you literary inspiration

Place my mind
Among the letters
Which make up the poet's name

Place my lines
There among their betters
Searching out for more of the same

That this time
Forceful with recrimination
Seeks dust to turn into dust

That the only crime
Besides falling for the musk
Is to remember naught of love

Shape then in the zero
A zen symbol
Towards a simpler life

Shape then for the hero
Towards a place beyond the strife
There to become all together closer

Within this blue
There are many colours

Within this ink
There are many compounds

Within this thought
There are many thoughts

Within this day
There are so so many days

Yet only one
Passage of time

Yet only one
Moment of moments

Yet only one
Place for recovery

Yet only one
Road to nowhere at all

My pen, filled with Berlin Blue
Already
You lift my mood

Without expectation
Or complication
You take me inside your truth

Where love
Is more than happy
Being there on its own terms

Looking out
Over curves and crescents
Remembering the moon once was the same

Just as that almost forgotten day
Sat by the canal in Amsterdam
Writing in my old new notebook

Already
You lift my mood
My pen, now filled with Berlin Blue

My blue blue pen
How many mistakes
Can a man make

How many opportunities
Might pass him by
How far into the distance

Should we try to see
How deep into the past
Ought this mind to wander

That I should ask you
My blue blue pen
To offer me your answers

No limit you say
To the mistakes
Or the opportunities

No limit you say
To distance, or depth
And for that I thank you

As I thank everyone
For the ink which flows
Through this blue blue pen

My book of blue
I turn to you
Before our poetry meet up

Coats of many colours
Worn by poets
Of so so many means

Some, for sure
Thinking to sit outside
On this fine summer's day

Others, like me
On a hanging landing
Or in a tiny, spare back room

With little wi-fi signal
And, possibly
Way less inspiration

To follow a coastline trace
With writings in Berlin Blue
To stroll from place to place
Betting each-way for a wider view

Going beyond the furthest feed
To seek out something new
Before the certain need
To know what it is which I find to be true

How many words would I write
How many thoughts might mine the strains
How my lack of movement or insight
Affects my old age aches and pains

The enquiry is sent by email
What might be the available choices
Springtime would be a good time to sail
Once again to hear those Hebridean voices

There is a blue
Which I desire to be with
A blue that might enter
My innermost thoughts

I will be free of distraction
Other than my own distractions

There is a blue
Though I am not certain
Exactly where to find you
Except that solitude might help

I shall be free of distraction
Other than my own distractions

There is a blue
Such that I may find as I venture
Under night stars and moonlight
Or step out into the midday sun

I wish for no distraction
Other than my own distractions

Alone now
Yet for how long I know not
Perhaps long enough

Most certainly
Time to write the word love
Then take it from there

September, Clumber Park, all are nourished
Around the longer corners
Into autumn, beyond winter

To write of sharp frosts
As well as Indian summers
To remember love

Through all of the seasons
From the first
Who you can't quite recall

To a later one
Who you often say
You won't ever, no, not ever forget

An escape from blue
That failure
To find, or detail
The forthcoming anew

A wayward association too
That fracture
To lose, or derail
The nestling few

An interest in the crew
Who scarper
To hoist, or raise the sail
As the jostling's due

A fairground inclination
The skylarker
To fly, or to curtail
The fossilising's skew

With my pen filled by blue
Here to record the impossible joy
To witness the fantasy of pain
Then to state, in a few words
All of why we live

That I pause, for thought
Highlights just where
The impossibilities are created
In that place before life
In that place after life

To remember footsteps
To recall handshakes
To cast back into the past
To lean forward into the future
With my pen filled by blue

My book of blue
I turn to you
In the heat
Of the summer

All way through
My book of blue
You turned me away
From becoming the runner

My book of blue
I learnt from you
Sitting here
On this fence of wonder

On clear days too
My book of blue
You joined the affray
To shred my pain asunder

The word is the word
From thought to pen
From now to then
From meditation to zen

The hope is the thought
From here and now
To slow down somehow
Before the shapely bough

The here is the way
Walking by my side
Waiting for the ride
All of that, and more beside

The walking is the step
It is what to take next
The way to clear the vexed
Written, as if one day to text

Not yet in the moment
Still with the daze
Or the doze of morning

A real shortage
Of blue today
The grey is in the ascendance

But the breeze blows
So things will change
Eventually

A day then for music
To lift the gloom
Perhaps a trip to *Coney Island*

My blue of blue
I have booked a School of Life class
How to be more sociable

I hope, in the fulness of time
That you will consider the decision
To have been worthwhile

As worthwhile perhaps
As the pen and ink
Which scratches its way

Onto the pages
Of this Berlin Notebook
Which was also a treasured purchase

Later, after breakfast
Or maybe I should say brunch
For it is after eleven already

Anyway, later I will iron
Iron those clothes which I bought
When in a similar mood

Berlin Blue ink in my Lamy pen
Neglected for many days
Following the tidying up
But found again now

Just in time
To prepare for a visit
To the car repair shop
And then on to Gibraltar Point

One to put a spring
Into the rear suspension
One to encourage a spring
Into these thin old legs

That I and my car
May go on
For many more miles
Before the harvest

Oh my blue book
And my blue pen
Is it fair to burden you
With my superficial
And, if I am able to recall them
With my deeper troubles

I write
Sat, in a comfortable lounge
In a more than adequate dwelling
Which is provided
By my loving, caring partner
Of course I do feel trapped

It is not my decision
How we proceed
It is not for me to choose
To sell up
And change our life completely
Yet that is what I think to do

Blue pen
Unshakeable
In the shaking hand

Untenable
In the tenant's
Fading grip

Unwavering
On the wave
Of the written line

Unbreakable
With the break in the prose
To allow the reader to take a break

Unenforceable
By the combined forces
Of time and tide

Undone
By the doings
Of the fathomable men

Unloved
By the lovers
Who let you go

So Blue
We've booked a table for tea

A few beers for sure
Who knows what else
Who knows who else
In these the oddest of times
Already, or so it seems
We are on vacation

How are we to be affected Blue
Where do you see things going

Are you optimistic
Are you confident
Should we reach out
To that creative space
Of heart and soul
Of truth and beauty

Oh Blue

Oh how so so easy

To write with you

Blue on my mind

Blue in my body

Blue with my soul

Oh blue

How neat

To be with you

To be on my mind

To be in my body

To be with my soul

Oh blue

How just right

To be near to you

You, on my mind

You, in my body

You, with my soul

Again I turn to you, Blue
Yet, by now I have reached
The perforated pages

Notes written there, are ready
For the plucking, or the pulling
Perhaps to send to a lover

Yet no lover
For this notelet, no
This one is for you, Blue

To tuck away
In your tuck-away feather bed
Of pasts and futures

That you, and you alone
Might take it on that longer journey
To the stars and the sequinned sisters

Blue book
On a North Pennines
Northumberland vacation

Chimneys on the moors
Blanket cows
By a windy Derwent reservoir

Sheep in the field
Outside the picture window
Of Finney Hill Green

One of us is out walking
Up and down the freedom hills
The other one is inside, consistently writing

La Belle Epoque
Mon Plaisir
Under grey skies
On this northern ridge

La Belle Epoque
Mon Plaisir
On the first Monday
Of September

La Belle Epoque
Mon Plaisir
Browsing the bulb catalogue
For flowers in May

Nowhere now
Nowhere
Ever before

Windblown clouds
Windblown trees
Hand built dry-stone walls

With moss and lichen
With damp and dew
With toppings turned

Not the time now
Not the time
Ever before

It is the love
It is the stain
To drive on by
To free the pain

It is but out there
Then back in here again
It is with love
I loved the rain

It is here and now
Not one to complain
I was with the love
I did not abstain

Take time to take time
Breathe, breathe one breath deeper
You do let go, you don't let go
Your mind cannot be
Your body's keeper

Make space to make space
Sing, sing one song sweeter
You don't let go, you do let go
Your blood cannot be
Your rhythm's seeker

Be present to be present
Share, share one share neater
You do, you don't, you do
Your soul cannot be
Your sorrow's reaper

I have found you
In these sheets of blue
I have found you
My love once turned through

I have sought you
So much at least is true
I have sought you
My love once torn through

I have hopes for you
With these lines I move
I have hopes for you
My love I once twisted through

The final page
Of Berlin Blue
In Nummer Eins
That is

But I have to say
That, my dearest
You will return
In Nummer Zwei

And again
Or so I do believe
Will be the same
In Nummer Drei